TO GRANDFATHER'S HOUSE WE GO

A Roadside Tour of American Homes

HARRY DEVLIN

TO GRANDFATHER'S HOUSE WE GO

A Roadside Tour of American Homes

To my daughter, Wende Elizabeth

FOUR WINDS PRESS NEW YORK

DUTCH COLONIAL

This house is the oldest house in the book. Until very recent times, descendants of the family who built the house have lived in it. It was built by Dutch colonists in 1664 and is very little changed since that time.

Most Dutch Colonial houses, no matter how small, have the same overhanging roof (architects call it *overshoot*) and are usually stone to above the first story. This house is made of cedar shingles and brownstone which were easily obtained by the New Jersey colonists.

A legend persists that the roof of this type of Dutch house extended over the body of the building to protect the masonry which in early days was cemented with clay and straw mortar. The legend doesn't explain why the gable ends were not also protected. The colonists probably adapted old designs from Flanders and Holland to remind themselves of home. They were good designs, because many houses today are built along similar lines.

Rembrandt was painting his last pictures when this house was built. It was originally on a huge tract of land overlooking Nieu Amsterdam (New York City). A few years ago, it was moved stone by stone from the city which had crowded around it to a suburban town twenty miles away.

Like Rembrandt's paintings, the house has never looked better, even though it was 199 years old when Lincoln made his Gettysburg address.

Dutch Colonial workman

OVERSHOOT

Gambrel roof with overshoot

Dutch farmhouse

WM. O'S PATTERN-ENDED HOUSE

A traveler passing near this lonely little house wouldn't be able to find even a footpath to its door. It is no longer lived in, but a spirited some-one has recently restored it to its original condition. Only a few years ago its gambrel roof was caved in, its windows gone and gaping holes spoiled the beautiful brickwork on the shadow side of this colonial house.

The gable end of the Wm. O house bears the owner's initials and the date of the completion of his house. A builder of that time and of that heritage sometimes added his wife's initials and floral or geometric patterns. The colonial builder was carrying on a tradition first brought to England by Flemish and Norman builders of the fifteenth century. The gambrel roof that earlier Dutch colonists used in their houses came from the same Flemish and Norman origins.

The initials are not the only interesting thing about Mr. Oakford's house. The doorway on the left has no stairs and no hinges. That door was used for one purpose and one purpose alone. On the occasion of a death in the household, the door was unscrewed and the coffin was pushed through the doorway to the waiting hearse wagon outside. The door was then screwed in place again, not to be reopened until the next sad occasion. In the same area, other similar houses have tiny "soul windows" where the O of Wm. O is. It was left open at the death of a householder so that the soul could make its exit.

But the best part of the house is its ghost. He's called the Alloway Ghost and he stalks the surrounding meadows and fields in his blue and buff patriot's uniform, carrying a pickax in a hopeless search for his lost treasure. It seems that one of William Oakford's descendants, on joining General Washington's army, buried his family silver in the cellar of this house. At the end of the war, the soldier, still in uniform, went directly to the cellar. Using a pickax, he began to dig for his treasure. He soon discovered that his silver had been stolen. Anguish and weariness, brought on by his frantic digging, were too much for the old soldier, and he died. The door was unscrewed for the last time and the Alloway Ghost soon came to haunt the lonely countryside.

The initials aren't painted. They were made of separate bricks, sur-faced with saltpeter and baked near an open fire until the surface became glassy and white.

The pattern end of a Pattern-Ended house

THE EARLY SETTLER HOUSE

In 1750 most Americans lived in houses like this. America had some cities where more elaborate houses stood, but the average American was a farmer and this was his home.

The house is very much like a log cabin in concept. But its lines, the sense of proportion, the handsome chimney and use of less crude materials, put it in the realm of architecture.

This farmhouse was built with hand-hewn beams cut from the surrounding forest, braced, mortised and trunneled by crude tools. It was then covered with hand-split shingles called shakes. The house was undoubtedly built by the original occupant. It was a house repeated with small variations all over the thirteen original states and it moved westward with the pioneers.

Early settlers had no time to waste on decorations. Their lives were hard, and practicality and efficiency were the guiding forces which dictated this kind of a house.

Beds were located around the central chimney for warmth. Sometimes smoke was allowed to seep into the attic where meats and fish could be smoked. The doorway led directly into the kitchen which was the center of activity for all of the busy family. Barns, built later, were often far larger than the house. If prosperity came to the family, sheds were added to the main house to accommodate activities or more family. Variations of the basic house shown were numerous. The saltbox house, with its long slanting extension, was one.

The house shown here is in a perfect state of preservation, thanks to the local historical society and the National Park Service. It is called the Wick House and was built by Henry Wick. In 1779-1780 it was the military quarters for Major General Arthur St. Clair, and it has a story. Young Tempe Wick was a not-too-patriotic miss whose horse meant more to her than the progress of the Revolution. Before General St. Clair took over the house, Tempe, for many months, was successful in keeping her horse away from American soldiers by hiding it in her bedroom. Somehow no one seemed too upset by this and Tempe survives in the story as a somewhat perverse heroine.

Tempe could have looked like this.

Saltbox

The log cabin preceded the Wick House.

GEORGIAN

Jacobean, Elizabethan, Queen Anne, Georgian and Victorian all describe periods in which English monarchs reigned. *Georgian* describes a long era in which a number of kings named George ruled England. George III was in charge when America gained its independence. Any literature, music, theatre and architecture of that era can be called Georgian. Technically, in America, a true Georgian house must have been built prior to the establishment of this nation's independence.

Houses for distinguished or wealthy American citizens were built by carpenters and master builders who usually followed drawings of houses already built in England. The prevalent style during the reign of the Georges was one which grew out of a combination of a number of influences largely classical in nature. The classical style was re-established by a brilliant Italian architect named Andrea Palladio (1508-80). The Palladian style was later carried to England by an architect with the fascinating name of Inigo Jones, who in turn inspired Christopher Wren and other architects with the Palladian feeling.

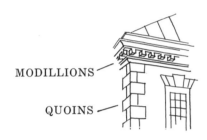

MODILLIONS

QUOINS

It is doubtful that the carpenter who built the mansion on the next page knew all this. He knew the style, he had builders' books and he knew how to make it look right. The wide boards used as siding were meant to look like the stone originals in England. The doorway and the windows over the doorway were called Palladian. You will see the same kind of windows in many houses and public buildings of this period. Even Independence Hall has Palladian windows.

The projections under the eaves are called *modillions,* and their history goes back to the time of the Greeks. Originally, Greek temples were built of wood, and the wooden rafters which supported the roof projected beyond the walls. In time the modillions became a decorative echo of the original rafter ends. Brackets are brackets in the same sense as a bracket which supports a shelf.

Palladian window

There are many panes in the windows because glass was difficult to manufacture in large sizes. Only after the 1860s could builders use larger windowpanes.

The Georgian house on the neighboring page is, with the exception of the porch, exactly as it was when it was built for Colonel Jacob Ford in 1774. In 1779-1780, General Washington used this house as his headquarters. It was the low ebb of American fortunes during the Revolution. But good news came here when General Lafayette arrived with word that France had become our ally and an army was coming to our aid. Colonel Ford died in the service of his country. The Ford mansion is cared for today by the National Park Service.

Georgian detail

It has been said that the robust Georgian is masculine while the Federal, with its delicate decoration, is feminine. Any generalization of this sort is risky, but could be helpful in your architectural detective work.

THE FEDERAL HOUSE

The Federal period of architecture (1790-1820) is so called because its birth and the birth of our nation were more or less simultaneous. The style is sometimes called Post-Colonial or Adamesque-Federal.

In 1784, a Scotsman named Robert Adam visited the ancient ruins and excavations at Herculaneum in Italy. Mr. Adam and his brother made drawings of many designs from the ruins and returned to classical-conscious England to start a style that the furniture designers, Mr. Sheraton and Mr. Chippendale, would further enrich. The design elements consisted of wreaths, wheat sheaves, fans, festoons and other ancient forms.

By the late eighteenth century the Adam style had crossed the ocean. Given subtle variations by native carpenters and architects, it emerged as our own Federal style, and soon houses of brick, stone or wood, with hip, gambrel and gable roofs appeared in all thirteen states. Carpenters took pride in making beautiful fan lights and delicate columns. Fireplaces, corner cupboards and other cabinetry showed the same concern. Many of the designs of the Georgian era were used, but with a delicacy not seen before.

The house shown here is a very simple house made elegant by its beautiful portico and the delicate dentil molding under the eaves. The columns are Doric with a Roman classical feeling. The transom light over the door is fan shaped and the side lights typically Adamesque.

Mount Vernon, although built in 1740, was extensively remodeled and enlarged by George Washington after the Revolution, and embodies much of the character of Federal architecture. Gracie Mansion, the home of the mayor of New York City, is another fine example of the Federal style.

Young lady of the time

*Gambrel-roofed Federal
with paired chimneys*

GREEK REVIVAL MANSION

Although this fine house was built almost three decades before the Greek Revival style became the dominant architectural direction in our country, it is a classic example of the style.

The columns (though square) and the pediment are Doric and express all the dignity of the ancient Greek temples which inspired the design. Front and back of the house are almost identical.

The deep white band beneath the eaves is called the entablature, and the decorations which look like little blocks of stone are known as a dentil mold.

Thomas Jefferson was a violinist, a president of the United States and a scholar. He was also an architect. His home, Monticello, is an example of Roman or Classical Revival. It differs from the Greek in that it utilizes the dome and other more involved forms. Greek architecture is characterized by simple basic forms and its bold directness led to its popularity in domestic architecture.

Classical or Roman Revival architecture was largely reserved for government buildings (the White House and the Capitol in Washington) and never really reached the popularity of the Greek Revival.

A French emigré built this house on one of General Washington's campsites in 1793. The bricks were made on the spot and mules carried marble for sills and fireplaces from a hundred miles away. There are hidden doors in the huge square columns that lead to underground hideaways for escaping slaves. At a later time, ammunition was stored nearby. A. B. Frost, the American humorist and illustrator, called this home towards the end of the nineteenth century.

Young lady of 1820

Simplified evolution of a Greek temple.

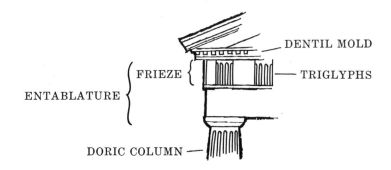

DENTIL MOLD

FRIEZE — TRIGLYPHS

ENTABLATURE

DORIC COLUMN

FARMER'S GREEK REVIVAL

The word *classic* comes from the Latin and it originally meant superior. Architecturally, it now refers to the building designs of the Greeks and Romans. When the classical architecture inspired by the Greeks was introduced to America in the 1820s, it was greeted with unusual enthusiasm.

America was beginning to feel its strength as a nation and many Americans felt that our spirit and system of government were a rebirth of the spirit of the ancient Greek Republic. Also, America was hostile towards Britain because of the burning of Washington and the other injuries to pride, person and property received during the War of 1812. Architectural imports continued, but the builders' books imported from England had to be Greek. To make matters more emotional, the contemporary Greeks were fighting a desperate war for independence from the Turks, and America was sympathetic.

Now towns formerly named for Biblical places were named for Greek cities and heroes. The existing states soon were graced with towns named Homer, Cicero, Attica, Sparta, Athens, Syracuse, Troy, etc.

Little Greek temples grew everywhere in the form of houses, churches, schools and public buildings. The revival lasted for thirty years and pushed south and westward with the expansion of our frontiers.

Visitors to our young nation were amazed—and amused—to find Greek temples in clearings where only months before Indians had lived. The visitors were also entertained by the fact that our little temple houses were made of wood instead of the traditional marble. The fact that original Greek temples were made of wood before they were built of stone didn't seem to affect the visitors' smiling indulgence.

This handsome Farmer's Greek Revival house has a noble feeling despite its deceptively small size. The passerby won't know that a false front covers a shed at the near side of the picture. The builder knew what he was doing. He gave the viewer an impression of dignity and serenity although it is really just a farmhouse with pillars and a pediment.

It shows what good grooming can do.

Young man of the time

When a pillar is flat against a house, it is called a pilaster.

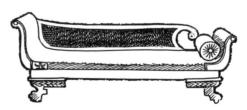

Empire-style sofa is Greek Revival.

VICTORIAN ROSETTA STONE

The year was 1883. Robert Louis Stevenson published *Treasure Island* and Mark Twain was polishing the last pages of *Huckleberry Finn*. Grandfather was so busy with the construction of his dream house that he almost missed the news of the war with the Apache Indians.

Grandfather didn't realize that he was building a house that would become a dictionary of Victorian styles. He thought of it only as romantic and wonderfully picturesque. He was willing to spend extra money for the tall chimneys and the fancy scrollwork.

Now, many years later, it is clear that the house is a fascinating example of Victorian Composite (or Eclectic). It is made of styles originating in France and Italy and uses ideas from European castles and cathedrals.

The decoration at the peak of the gable is known as a finial, while the one hanging below is a pendant. Finials and pendants are often repeated inside the house, around stairways and fireplaces and as decorations on Victorian furniture.

The fancy scrollwork inside the gable is called bargeboarding (or vergeboards). If the bargeboards have a design that looks like vines or flowers, they are then called foliated bargeboards.

When the gutters level out from the roof and are supported by brackets, the detail is called Italianate.

The boxlike roof at the shadow side of the house is a Mansard roof and the pattern of the bricks in the chimney gives a feeling of the battlements of a castle. The hood molding over the front windows and the diamond panes in the upper window are from Tudor constructions.

The first floor window has a pair of pointed arches separated by a trefoil at the top. (A narrow window with a pointed arch is called a lancet.)

The front of the house is sheathed in board-and-batten sheathing. The board is the wide part, the batten the narrow.

The house has elements of Gothic, Mansard, Italianate and Embattled architecture, the four styles that dominated the nineteenth century after the decline of Greek Revival. If there was a style around, Grandfather didn't want to neglect it.

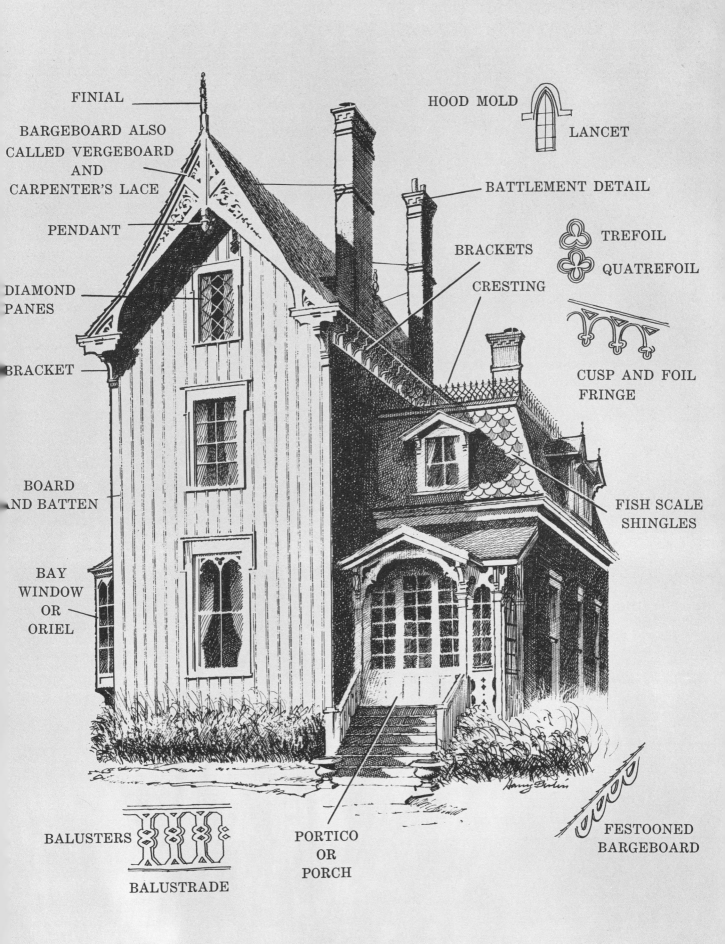

FINIAL

HOOD MOLD

BARGEBOARD ALSO
CALLED VERGEBOARD
AND
CARPENTER'S LACE

LANCET

BATTLEMENT DETAIL

PENDANT

BRACKETS

TREFOIL

QUATREFOIL

CRESTING

DIAMOND
PANES

CUSP AND FOIL
FRINGE

BRACKET

FISH SCALE
SHINGLES

BOARD
AND BATTEN

BAY
WINDOW
OR
ORIEL

BALUSTERS

PORTICO
OR
PORCH

FESTOONED
BARGEBOARD

BALUSTRADE

HANSEL AND GRETEL GOTHIC

The Brooklyn Bridge is Gothic, too.

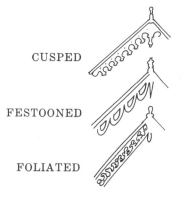

CUSPED

FESTOONED

FOLIATED

Bargeboards

In 1747, an English author, Horace Walpole, built a Gothic "castle" for his country home and called it Strawberry Hill. True, there were many castles in Europe that were being lived in, but his home was probably the first one to be built in imitation of a castle. It marked the beginning of the Gothic Revival in architecture which would reach its peak a hundred years later in the mid-nineteenth century.

This little house is a variation of American Gothic. It is sometimes called Swiss Gothic, sometimes Chalet Gothic. Gothic it is and by one of America's greatest architects!

It was built in 1858 as a lodge for a church cemetery by James Renwick, who went on to build Grace Church and St. Patrick's Cathedral in New York City, Vassar College up the Hudson in Poughkeepsie, and the Smithsonian Institution in Washington.

It has remained unchanged since the day it was built and lacks only board-and-batten siding to be a dictionary of the Gothic Revival in America. It has pointed eaves with foliated (flowered) bargeboards; it has pendants and finials, picturesque chimneys and diamond-paned windows with Tudor hood moldings. The patterned roof and the braced overhanging balcony show a lot going on for a five-room house.

Our Hansel and Gretel house reflects more of the feeling of medieval Europe than others. Many medieval towns were walled to protect them from savage invaders. Houses had to grow upwards because of the lack of space inside the walls. Mr. Renwick's tiny house has plenty of room around it, but the cramped, hunched, medieval look was what the great architect wanted for his solitary cemetery house.

Architecture, music, literature and dress were all romantic in this time.

Strawberry Hill

GOTHIC REVIVAL RECTORY HOUSE

The first examples of Gothic Revival appeared in America as early as 1820. Almost all the styles that found acceptance here were revival forms that had first become fashionable in Europe. There, the Gothic style never had to be revived because it had never really died. In some form it remained an on-going style of architecture from its beginnings in the twelfth century. The new popularity of the Gothic style in Europe came from a new awareness of its romantic qualities. It was antique, nostalgic and, above all, romantic.

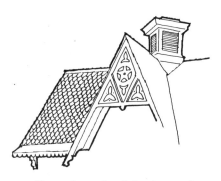

Bargeboard with unusual star and trefoil motif

By 1850 Gothic cottages were everywhere. They were built as work-men's simple homes and as millionaires' mansions. Colleges and churches were built in imitation of Gothic cathedrals in Europe. Neo-Gothic archi-tects argued that churches should no longer be built like Greek temples. After all, the ancient Greeks were pagans, while the Gothic church was Christian. By 1865 the Greek Revival, which had dominated architecture in America, had gone the way of all fashion.

The striking house shown here is the rectory to a beautiful board-and-batten Gothic church. The house has horizontal siding because the architect, Harrison Condit, felt that the house looked vertical enough. The handsome bargeboarding uses the quatrefoil (four lobes or circles) which symbolizes the cross. In the great house on the following two pages, the quatrefoil is used in the long balustrade which runs across the front. A trefoil (three lobes) medallion under the center eave symbolizes the Trinity.

Bargeboard variation

Mr. Condit's Gothic rectory uses many of the exterior features in-side the house. The stairway and fireplaces have their pendants, trefoils, quatrefoils and cusps. Each passing year makes a house like this more of a treasure.

PRINCESS HOUSE

The great brownstone house with the terra cotta roof which follows is yet another form of American Gothic. It has pointed, arched windows which is one of the distinguishing marks of Gothic architecture. The looping bargeboards, the pointed eaves and the heavy hood molds all give Gothic character.

It's a house fit for a princess. A real princess agreed and she lived here for almost thirty years. The glass building to the right is called an orangery. It's tall enough to grow orange and other fruit trees.

By the end of the Civil War in 1865, the Gothic Revival was in its last days. The Italianate and Mansard style had come to stay for a while.

THE OCTAGON HOUSE

Onion dome

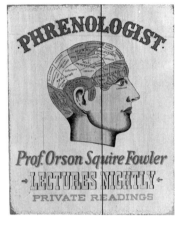

Phrenology was the "science" of the lumps on the head.

Domed octagon

In 1854 Orson Squire Fowler wrote a book called *A Home For All, or the Octagonal Style of Building*. He wrote indignantly that the Gothic, Italianate and Greek Revival houses being built were for the wealthy and privileged, but hardly suited to the average man. The fact that Mr. Fowler's chief reputation was as a phrenologist and not an architect never detracted from the popularity of his book.

Fowler's book was published at a time when America was delighted with all things scientific and pseudo-scientific. The octagon house was presented as a scientific answer to America's housing needs. It was claimed that the octagon was efficient, healthful and a form endorsed by nature. And after all, circles enclose more space with less wall and a dodecagon (twelve sides) or octagon was very close to a circle.

Soon octagon and dodecagon and circular houses were appearing wherever the spirit of science and adventure was strong enough to resist the outraged stares of hostile neighbors. By 1857 a builder's manual by I. Baker showed octagon houses, barns, schools, churches and public buildings. America had at last created its very own form of architecture! Octagons had formed towers of buildings and Mr. Palladio had used the octagon as a basic plan for some of his villas, but the simple octagon house was an American invention.

The quietly handsome little octagon shown here was built in 1865 by the town's postmaster, and he paid $450 for the house. The rooms are not pie-shaped as might be imagined, but are rectangular. The triangles left over were used as pantries, closets, bathrooms, etc. The plans shown below are typical of a small octagon house. The chimney is in the center of the house, radiating heat throughout.

In other parts of the country, some beautiful octagons were built in mansion form with gold onion-shaped domes and other elaborate decorations that undoubtedly made Orson Squire Fowler wonder if he'd ever quite made his point.

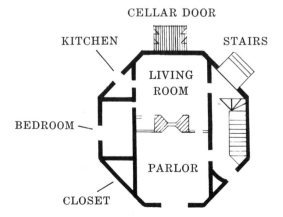

First floor

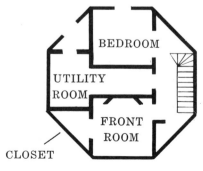

Second floor

THE ITALIANATE BROWNSTONE

Brownstone features

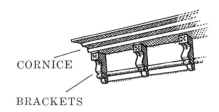

CORNICE

BRACKETS

LINTEL OR
HOOD MOLD

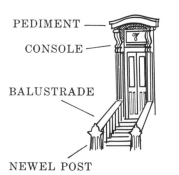

PEDIMENT

CONSOLE

BALUSTRADE

NEWEL POST

In Italian, the word *campanilismo* describes anyone with too much local pride. The word came into being because of the rivalry of Renaissance Italian towns and cities competing to build the most imposing bell tower or *campanile* (camp-an-*ee*-luh).

The most famous campanile is in Pisa. It leans. Though the Leaning Tower of Pisa is famous, it is not altogether typical. The common variety is square and tall with a flat or almost-flat roof, arched "windows" and projecting eaves with supporting brackets.

The elements of the campanile were imported by Americans as early as 1825 and continued in favor in one form or another as late as 1880.

Wealthy Americans making the Grand Tour of Europe in the 1840s were thoroughly impressed by the romantic qualities of Italian architecture. The fact that the most romantic personalities in the world of music and literature were associated with Italy at that time helped to impress visiting Americans so that the image they brought home simply had to find expression in their new houses. Our enterprising carpenters and builders knew just what to do.

The big city brownstone house is really an imitation of one side of a campanile. Although the windows are often rectangular, the hoods over the windows suggest the rounded tops of the arches of the campanile. The tall, narrow shape and the flat bracketed eaves continue the likeness.

The lonely brownstone opposite now looks quite antique in the company of its modern neighbors. It once had identical neighbors, numbering in the hundreds of thousands. The wrecker's ball and ambitious remodelers have thinned the ranks of the brownstone Italianates, but a new appreciation of the style has rescued them in many cities. Brownstone associations have been formed and it is now possible to buy replacement consoles, brackets and cornices for ailing Italianates.

*These three poets helped to
make the image of Italy romantic.*

SHELLEY

KEATS

BYRON

ITALIANATE TUSCAN VILLA

By the late 1840s, some of the enthusiasm for all things Greek had cooled. The Gothic and the Italianate forms of architecture were becoming increasingly fashionable. A strong feeling for things romantic had fired the tastes of our country. The fanciful novels by Edgar Allan Poe, the pastoral paintings of Thomas Cole, and the sentimental music and poetry of the time all contributed to the desire of Americans to build romantically. Bell towers, pointed gables and castellations gave Grandfather a chance to express his particular brand of imaginative romanticism. Many chose the Italianate as did the builder of the house opposite.

Status was another feeling Grandfather wanted to express. Like his Italian campanilismo counterpart, he built as high and as bracketed as he could to let everyone see what a success he was.

The cupola on this house is really the topmost extension of a campanile which is an integral part of the house. Cupolas (they are sometimes called belvederes) are largely useless and usually kept sealed off to conserve heat. But they were a must for anybody who was anybody in the '60s, '70s and '80s.

The Italianate is the favorite form of architecture for directors of ghost movies. Perhaps because these houses are often surrounded by huge trees or because their locations silhouette them against the sky, they have gained a haunted look. But high ceilings, windows that sometimes extend to the floor, and generous moldings and decorations actually make the Italianates cheerful places to live and wonderful houses for children to grow up in.

Modernizing a house is not a new idea. Many colonial houses were "modernized" to look Italianate by the addition of brackets under the eaves and even the addition of a campanile. The sketch below shows just what can happen when an unsuspecting farmhouse falls victim to Victorian modernization.

In many parts of the country this kind of house is called a Tuscan Villa house and, of course, Victorian.

An Italian Campanile

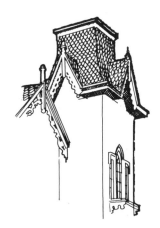

Italianate campanile with Gothic details

AMERICAN EMBATTLED OR CASTELLATED

Grandfather in 1882

Castles originally were strongholds to protect inhabitants from hostile soldiers. Slit windows (lancets) were not for ventilation. They were designed so that archers could ventilate their enemies. High walls were built to discourage any thought of scaling them and the battlements were designed to give the defenders a good shot at the invaders. Machicolations, which were slits built out from the battlements, were planned so that the home team could drop hot oil on the men with the ladders. Castles were very functional.

That Grandfather wasn't threatened by Black Knights had nothing to do with the fact that Grandfather was in love with castles and everything they represented—troubadors, secret cloisters and coats-of-arms. Ivanhoe was very much in his mind.

When he could afford a castle, Grandfather built it. He needed a hill so that the castle's silhouette would impress the passerby as much as possible. The insides were wood paneled and full of Gothic trefoils, cusps and other forms probably copied from a coronation throne.

Castles were built by the hundreds and made skylines romantic for many areas of the nation, but like the original structures, they were uncomfortable places to live in. The high cost of heating and repair has accounted for the destruction of many of the castles. The remaining few serve as monuments to Grandfather's love of romance.

This castle was first built in 1871, the year that the great Chicago fire destroyed 17,450 buildings. Not long after, a fire destroyed our castle, but in 1882 it was rebuilt in stone and brick to intrigue anyone who has inherited Grandfather's romantic feelings.

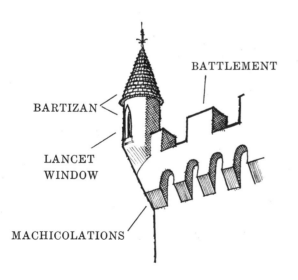

BARTIZAN

BATTLEMENT

LANCET
WINDOW

MACHICOLATIONS

*Not all American castles
are king-size.*

MANSARD HOUSE

At any time of day, this Mansard house has character. In the hours near dusk, a traveler sees more than a house—he sees romance. The romantic era produced the Gothic, the Italianate and the Greek Revival, among others, but the Mansard was *French* romantic and it hit America hard. Isolated examples were built in the early 1850s, but the style was in full fashion by 1870. Hotels, college dormitories, church rectories and houses of every size adopted the characteristic Mansard roof. The Mansard roof was almost always slate, but a few survivors still show shingles.

In 1598, François Mansart was born in Renaissance France. He was destined to become a great architect but a failure as a person. He was headstrong and arrogant and not scrupulously honest. Worse, he was a spendthrift with his clients' money. He once ordered a wing of a massive building to be torn down because it offended his eye. His client thought Monsieur Mansart's eye should have been offended during the drawing-board stage.

François Mansart's genius brought classicism in architecture to France and he popularized what is now known as the Mansard roof. But he spent the last ten years of his life without a commission.

The Mansard roof is often used in storefronts of contemporary buildings. It has found favor in many variations of twentieth century architecture, but the Mansard era was the nineteenth century and the romantic houses that go by that name fortunately survive in great numbers. Some art historians refer to the Mansard house as Franco-American, but Grandfather called it Mansard.

A surge of friendship towards the French helped establish the popularity of the Mansard house. Lafayette was still a great hero in the 1870s. Soon the Statue of Liberty, a gift from the people of France, was to be unveiled (1886). And America was, at that time, fond of any fellow revolutionists.

Mansard doorway

Mansard variations

FRANCO ITALIANATE

Eclecticism wasn't limited to vacation houses. All across America builders scrambled the styles into ingenious combinations: Neo-Jacobean and Romanesque, simple farmhouses with elaborate campaniles, Gothic with the Italianate, and other combinations too numerous and sometimes too hideous to mention.

Many of the combinations, however, have a warmth and charm that purists choose to ignore. This handsome house, built in 1875, combines a Mansard roof with a campanile straight from Italy. The fish-scale shingles at the top of the tower indicate that the designer was aware of the beginning of new trends towards texture. The iron cresting along the rooftops is also textural.

The house is still impressive, but only to eyes and brains that can relate to what the builder had in mind. In 1875 the house was impressive to everyone. The spirit of campanilismo had come to another American town.

At the side of the campanile is a round window in which there is red glass. People inside the campanile can look out, but the glass is opaque to anyone looking in.

The son of the man who owns the house had his own radio station here. Reception was wonderful.

Only towards the second half of the nineteenth century were architects licensed. Most people who built houses were contractors or carpenters who followed the plans published in builders' manuals. In the early nineteenth century many of these builders' guides were imported from England. American styles were generally ten to twenty years behind English styles. In Ohio, a style could be five to ten years behind the New York or Massachusetts styles.

Builders and carpenters used the imported manuals as guides, but often made shrewd variations. The use of American materials and American ingenuity created styles that were distinctively American. The house on the cover of this book is one of the most distinctive. It's one of a kind and a joy in a world full of architectural mass production. Its owners, aware of its value, care for it like a fine violin or a rare manuscript.

An architectural melange—
octagonal campanile,
Italianate eaves, Mansard
roof and some bargeboards
for good measure

NEO-JACOBEAN

In 1870 a new kind of architectural form was introduced to America. This time the inspiration came from England where a revival of a style that was fashionable during the reign of James I was in full flower.

Jacobus is Latin for James. James I became King of England in 1603 after the death of Queen Elizabeth I. Furniture, literature, architecture and other arts of the time are called Jacobean. The style which American builders imported and Americanized is correctly called Neo-Jacobean.

Even though there are thousands of Neo-Jacobean houses, they are rarely called by that name. The son of the builder of the great house on the two pages following called the style Queen Anne. Others think of it and the little white house opposite as an Eastlake style. Most people just call them Victorian, which is safe if nothing else.

The steam-driven scroll saw which cut the miles of decorated bargeboards for the "gingerbread" effects on the Gothic and Italianate houses was now replaced by the lathe. Spindles and shingles were "in" and board and batten were "out." Textured surfaces, fish-scale shingles and strapwork became the builders' delight.

The white house opposite has many of the hallmarks of the Neo-Jacobean. The columns which support the roof of the porch and porte-cochere have an inverted look. The tower, with its medieval cresting ornament, and the spindles under the eaves of the porch contribute to the fashion. The great house on the following pages was finished in 1883 (the same year that the Brooklyn Bridge, a Gothic structure, was completed). The chimneys, the strapwork, the fanciful shingles and the general English seventeenth century feeling are all Neo-Jacobean.

In a few years, the Neo-Jacobean style often merged with the Romanesque. Some houses were Romanesque in the stone first story and Neo-Jacobean in the wooden second floor. Rough stones, patterned shingles, grillwork and acres of spindles kept American craftsmen busy in the last years of the nineteenth century.

Some Neo-Jacobean hallmarks

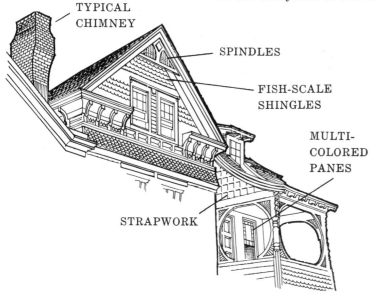

TYPICAL CHIMNEY

SPINDLES

FISH-SCALE SHINGLES

MULTI-COLORED PANES

STRAPWORK

Young man of the Neo-Jacobean Era

THE ECLECTIC VACATION HOUSE

Eclectic means the gathering together of various systems or elements, and this house is exuberantly eclectic. The pointed eaves with the fancy bargeboards are Gothic; the little circular tower has an Oriental quality; the fish-scale shingles remind us of the Neo-Jacobean. Finally, the flat eaves and the brackets at the porch roof are Italianate. People would more likely use the word *gingerbread* in referring to this kind of house.

The seashore town that this white house graces has made a wise effort to preserve its gingerbread-era houses and hotels. Grandfather's vacation house expresses a feeling of play and exhilaration that must have made the long trip by smoky train worth all the trouble.

Whoever designed the house threw caution to the winds and put together elements that would have shocked the sensibilities of a previous generation. Tastes had changed and eclecticism was no longer a bad word.

All over our country, near great lakes and rivers and at the seashores, high-spirited houses, similar to this one, reflected the owners' optimism and individuality. Grandfather must have had a wonderful time.

A contemporary of the Eclectic Vacation house

ROMANESQUE

The great Roman Empire took a long time to fall. When it finally did, late in the fifth century, it took art and architecture with it. For the next several hundred years no new western style emerged to rival the grandeur of Rome. By the eleventh century western man had pulled himself together sufficiently to develop a recognizable and effective architecture. The basic design was Roman, but adapted to the rugged and perilous life of the Middle Ages. Romanesque architecture, as it is called, became the standard for churches, abbeys, castles and other buildings during those troubled times. It was also the architecture from which the well-known Gothic style would spring.

The Romanesque style is characterized by rounded arches, squat columns and massive, crudely cut (rusticated) blocks of stone. Round corner towers with conical roofs were more for protection from Vikings and other menaces than for decoration.

One thing distinguishes the Romanesque Revival from all the previous revivals. It began here. All previous revivals began in Europe and found favor here fifteen or twenty years later.

Henry Hobson Richardson was largely responsible for the introduction of the Romanesque in 1876. He built churches, libraries and residences in this style and then went on to create a style which bridged into concepts of modern (twentieth century) architecture.

Although built late in the nineteenth century, Romanesque houses are already scarce. They have gone the way of many of the great houses of the Victorian era. Because they were usually located on corner lots, they have in many instances been sacrificed for new apartment houses. Others have been destroyed to recover the cut stone of which they were usually made.

One day, some years ago, the author was walking down a street in New York. In an open book in a bookshop window he noted ". . . when children grow up, they should have something left around them that's worth looking at . . . buildings that will give them a sense of continuity with the past . . . houses that have figured in history, sheltered a genius, helped nurture generations of families, or just been the haunt of a ghost."

The house shown here is doomed. A housing project will destroy it and the romantic Italian Renaissance house beside it. At the time of writing, all the other houses in this book are standing, and in no immediate danger of destruction, but the same cannot be said of their companions. Every day, yet another fine old house falls to the wreckers. It is your heritage that is being displaced, not just homeless ghosts.

Squat columns, heavy arches,
rough stone, corner towers and fanciful
roof lines are all Romanesque.

THE ALL-AMERICAN LITTLE RED SCHOOLHOUSE

This last house is the only house in the book that is not a house to live in. It is a one-room schoolhouse and the fifth grade of a very modern school system which houses the other grades in very modern school buildings. That the children of the fifth grade hate to go on to the sixth is a tribute to its warm and cheery good looks.

Although the building with its gable roof and straight sides seems to be a very simple example of the Little Red Schoolhouse, a number of influences give it character.

The brackets under the eaves are Italianate. The white trim which follows the eaves forms a pediment to remind us of Greek Revival. The triangles over the windows are a carpenter's version of Gothic Revival. Even the color is imported. American barn red is the color that the farmers of Sweden have painted their barns and houses for centuries.

Only the tepee and possibly the octagon house can be said to be one hundred per cent American architecture. Every other architectural style has come from other, older lands. But like all things American, the styles soon developed American character and the Little Red Schoolhouse, like apple pie, became a symbol of something jubilantly American.

ADDENDUM

The term Grandfather is used loosely. A generation is usually judged as a thirty-three-year period. If we were to use that kind of a yardstick, our grandfather who built the Dutch house would be a great-great-great-great-great-great-great-great-grandfather!

The houses in this book are but a sampling of the diversified styles of architecture that characterized the American scene, but their counterparts can be found almost anywhere in the United States. True, the Dutch Colonial you will see in California may be newer than your second teeth, but its antecedents go back to the ancient house that opens this book. The East Coast is the richest, architecturally speaking, as it was the first to feel each new wave of fashion as it came from Europe. It so happens that all but two of the houses discussed are located in New Jersey which was a cultural crossroads—East and West, North and South—for anything new that came along. Whatever architectural fancy that rode down the pike found expression in this state. However, it is interesting to see how the later waves swept farther and farther inland as the Middle West and Far West opened up. The Federal style, for instance, was already waning as Ohio was settled, and the crest of Greek Revival did not get much beyond the Mississippi, whereas the Gothic Revival, Italianate and later styles appear with variations all the way to the West Coast.

Specifically regional styles, such as Spanish Mission and Western Ranch, have not been dealt with here as they are not as characteristic of the American scene as the houses depicted. All the houses shown are as they are today. They were chosen because they represent houses of their kind and are largely unchanged from the time they were built.

The house on the cover of this book is composed of a variety of imported architectural styles, combined with such skill and ingenuity that the blend defies any usual definition. This house is a tribute to nineteenth century American imagination and might be called *American Exuberant*.

Library of Congress Cataloging in Publication Data
Devlin, Harry.
  To grandfather's house we go.
  SUMMARY: Presents 22 styles of American homes popular at various periods in our history.
  1. Architecture, Domestic—United States—Juvenile literature. [1. Architecture, Domestic. 2. Dwellings] I. Title.
NA7205.D53 1980 728.3'7'0973 80-15294 ISBN 0-590-07764-3

Published by Four Winds Press
A division of Scholastic Magazines, Inc., New York, N.Y.
Copyright © 1967 by Harry Devlin
All rights reserved
Printed in the United States of America
Library of Congress Catalog Card Number: 80-15294
1 2 3 4 5 84 83 82 81 80

To Rev. James Elliott Lindsley and all the knowledgeable people who helped me in the research of this book, I express my appreciation.